KRIK?
KRAK!

Amy Crofford

BEACON HILL PRESS

OF KANSAS CITY

Copyright 2008
by Beacon Hill Press of Kansas City

Printed in the United States of America

ISBN: 978-0-8341-2367-0

Cover Design: Darlene Filley
Illustrator: Robyn Jorde
Inside Design: Sharon Page

Editor: Donna Manning
Assistant Editor: Allison Southerland

Note: These true stories of missionaries and their work in Haiti
are conveyed through the fictional characters of a grandfather
and his grandchildren. It is part of the *Kidz Passport to Mis-*
sions curriculum.

10 9 8 7 6 5 4 3 2 1

Dedication

To the many people who have worked in Haiti,
Missionaries and volunteers,
For a day or a decade,
Not all could be mentioned here.
But God knows,
And the work continues.
Thank you!

Contents

1. School Days   7

2. Merry Christmas   12

3. Grandma Yvette Is Sick   16

4. God Is the Best Doctor   21

5. Thank a Teacher   25

6. Sitting Snake   30

7. God's World   33

8. Busy Hands and Full Stomachs   38

9. From Here to There   43

10. New Churches   47

11. God Answers Prayer   52

1
School Days

"Please tell us a story!" Sadrack, Marie, and Esther begged, as they ran to give their grandpa a hug. Every day after school, the children went to their grandparents' house until their parents could pick them up and take them home.

"Now children, you know work comes before story time. Tell me what you learned in school today," encouraged Grandpa Lucien [loo-see-EN].

"I learned that Christopher Columbus discovered Haiti [HAY-tee] on December 6, 1492," said Sadrack. "He called our island Hispaniola, or Little Spain."

"Good! Marie, what about you?"

"My teacher said that we must wear shoes. They keep little worms from getting into our skin through the bottoms of our feet."

"That's right," said Grandpa. "Esther, what did you learn?" asked Grandpa.

"I heard a riddle about a president."

"Tell us," said Sadrack.

"It is very small, but it wakes up the president from his sleep. Do you give up?" asked Esther, jumping up and down.

"Yes, we give up," said Marie.

"A bedbug!"

"That's funny," said Grandpa Lucien, "but what did you learn today?"

Esther frowned. "I can tell you what I didn't learn—this long list of French words. They're hard! Why do I have to learn French anyway?"

"You must learn French so you can talk to people from other countries," explained Grandpa.

"And to help you get a good job," added Sadrack.

"But I can speak Creole [KREE-ohl] (a blend of

French and West African languages). That's the language most Haitians speak," said Esther.

"But you need to learn French," Marie insisted. "I can help you."

"After you learn French, you can learn English or Spanish." Sadrack loved to tease his younger sister.

"No way!" Esther exclaimed. She thought for a minute. Then she smiled and said, "I can say one thing in French."

"What's that?" asked Grandpa Lucien.

"Moi, j'ai faim [MWAH, zhay FAHN]."

"That figures," said Sadrack. "You're always hungry!"

"I'm a growing girl," said Esther.

"Your grandma has a snack prepared for later," said Grandpa.

"Yeah!" cheered Esther.

"Grandpa, what about our story?" asked Marie.

"Do you have schoolwork?" he asked.

"No," said Sadrack. "I finished my work at school."

"I have math," said Marie.

"I have that long list of . . ."

"Esther, I'll help you with your French after I finish math, OK?"

"Thank you, Marie," said Grandpa. "Sadrack, you and I are going to build a bench while the girls do their homework."

Grandpa Lucien began sawing boards outside under the mango tree. While Grandpa used his saw to cut the boards, Sadrack asked a neighbor if he could borrow a hammer. Next, Sadrack went to the market to buy some nails. When Sadrack returned, his grandpa had the boards sanded and ready to nail together. It was hot work, even in the shade.

As the girls pulled out pens and paper from their backpacks, Marie smiled. Math was easy for her, and she would soon be done. Esther wrote and rewrote her list. When Marie quizzed her, she made a few mistakes. So they practiced again—this time with no mistakes.

"See, that wasn't so bad, was it?" asked Marie.

"I guess not. Let's see if Grandma needs our help."

The girls put away their schoolwork and went to find Grandma Yvette. "Can we help you with anything?" asked Marie.

"Yes, there are two thirsty people who have been working on a bench," said Grandma. "Would you please give them these glasses of citronade [SI-truh-nade] (a fruit drink similar to lemonade)? Then come back, and I'll give you some."

After everyone enjoyed a cool drink, the children said, "Grandpa, tell us a story."

"All right," said Grandpa Lucien. "Come sit on the bench. First, I want to thank you for your help today. Many hands make light work."

"Grandpa, we like to help you and Grandma," said Marie. Sadrack and Esther nodded.

"What story would you like to hear?" asked Grandpa Lucien. He turned over a large, empty paint pail and sat on it.

"Tell us about the beginning of the church here in Haiti."

"Oh, you want a story about Pastor Paul and his wife Mary?"

"Yes!" said Sadrack.

"But there are so many stories. They were missionaries here for 14 years, and Pastor Paul came back to visit several times. Which story should I tell?"

"I know," said Marie. "Tell us about their first Christmas here in Haiti."

"Yeah!" Esther and Sadrack said together.

Grandpa Lucien waited for the children to give him their complete attention. Then he asked, "Krik [KRIK]?"

The children knew that meant, "Are you ready to listen to a story?"

2
Merry Christmas

"Krak [KRAK]!" the children exclaimed.

Grandpa knew they were ready to listen. "Good!" he said. "Then let's begin. Pastor Paul and Mary Orjala [or-YAH-luh] arrived in Haiti on October 3, 1950. They knew that the most important thing they had to do was to learn French and Creole, so they could communicate with us. Then they could begin to teach us. They wanted to teach people who were called to be pastors. The pastors could then help the churches to grow. By Christmas, Pastor Paul and Mary could only say a few words in our language.

"On Christmas Eve day, Mary called, 'Paul, Paul, come quickly!' She could not believe her eyes. A man was selling Christmas trees. Paul and Mary had brought all of their lights and decorations with them, but they had not seen any trees yet. Now here was a man selling one at their door! Paul paid about 60 cents to buy a four-foot tree for the church.

"But when Paul and Mary arrived at the church, they found that the pastor had already decorated a tree. So they took their tree home and trimmed it with their decorations and lights.

"The tree made it seem more like Christmas. Pastor Paul and Mary had seen other signs of Christmas in Haiti too. Can you guess what they were?"

"The lanterns," guessed Esther.

"Yes, they had never seen anything quite so amazing," replied Grandpa.

"I like to make lanterns, but the ones I make are simple," said Marie.

"Did you see the one at the church last year?" asked Sadrack. "It must have taken hours for someone to cut the windows and doors out of the cardboard."

"And what about all the different colors of tissue paper glued in them!" said Esther.

"It was so beautiful with the candle shining from the inside," added Sadrack.

"It was beautiful, but there were other things that reminded Pastor Paul and Mary of Christmas," said Grandpa. "They were surprised to see poinsettias [poin-SET-uhs] in bloom when they traveled up the mountain. They had never seen a poinsettia plant that was taller then they were."

"The poinsettias are big!" exclaimed Esther. "Way bigger than I am!"

Grandpa Lucien chuckled and then continued his story. "It was time for Paul and Mary to go to the Christmas Eve service. Pastor Paul played the accordion, and it was awesome! It was the first time he had played in a service here in Haiti."

"Did he play other instruments too?" asked Marie.

"Yes, he played other instruments and also wrote songs. Do you know the song that says 'Nazarenes, wake up. It's time for us to preach the truth'?" asked Grandpa.

"Of course. We love that song!" said Sadrack and Esther.

"It was written by Pastor Paul," said Grandpa.

"Wow!" said Marie.

"What did Pastor Paul give Mary for Christmas?" asked Esther. Her mind was full of ideas.

"They didn't give presents to each other that first year," said Grandpa.

"Why not?" asked Marie.

"There was a pastor who needed a saddle blanket for his horse. And a pastor's wife needed to see a doctor because she was going to have a baby. There were so many needs that Pastor Paul and Mary spent their Christmas money on the Haitian people."

"That was nice," said Marie.

"Do you know the proverb (an old saying that tells a truth), 'Rocks in the water don't know the misery of the rocks in the sun'?"

"What does it mean, Grandpa?" asked Esther.

"Pastor Paul and Mary had never been in a poor country before. They had to learn that our culture (way of life) was different from what they were used to. They learned that they couldn't help everyone they wanted to help," explained Grandpa Lucien. "But God encouraged them in other ways. Every time the mail was delivered, they got another note from friends saying that they were praying for them. They even got notes from strangers saying that they were praying for them. God gave them courage and love through other people.

"On Christmas Day, Pastor Paul and Mary went to the church for a children's program. Later, they went to a friend's house for dinner and conversation. Pastor Paul and his wife had made many friends with missionaries from other groups. They asked questions and learned that some of their ideas were good, and some were not so good. By talking with other people, they avoided making many mistakes. They also set goals for the Church of the Nazarene in Haiti."

"What goals?" asked Esther.

"Pastor Paul wanted everyone to learn how to read the Bible in Creole. But not everyone could go to school, so they decided to have reading classes in the churches."

"Is that why so many Nazarene churches in Haiti have schools?" asked Marie.

"Yes, that's how they began. Another goal Pastor Paul had was to train Haitians how to pastor their own churches."

"Did Pastor Paul and Mary start the Bible college too?" asked Sadrack.

"Yes, they started it exactly one year after arriving in Haiti. They began with two classes and eight students. They thought that it was the most important thing they could do in Haiti."

"Oh," interrupted Esther, "our parents are here."

"Bye, Grandpa! Thanks for the story," said the children as they gathered up their backpacks.

"We want another story tomorrow," called Marie.

3
Grandma Yvette Is Sick

"Hi, Grandpa!" said Esther.

"Grandpa," called Sadrack, "look what I made!"

"Shhh! Your grandma is sleeping."

"What's wrong, Grandpa?" asked Marie. "Is she sick?"

"She must be sick. She never goes to sleep when she knows we're coming," whispered Sadrack.

"Yes, she's sick. She tossed and turned all night with a high fever and chills," explained Grandpa. "She said her head hurt so badly that any noise or light was painful. She couldn't eat either."

"What's wrong with Grandma?" asked Esther, looking worried.

"She has malaria [muh-LAIR-ee-uh] (a disease that a person gets from a mosquito bite)," Grandpa replied.

"Esther and I can help get dinner ready for you, Grandpa," volunteered Marie.

"Yeah, we can do that," added Esther eagerly.

"Thanks, girls," replied Grandpa Lucien, "but your mom is bringing some rice and beans for our dinner."

"Is there anything we can do?" asked Esther.

"Well, you could make some juice for her. That would be good."

Esther went to get the little citrons. Some were yellow, but most were green. Marie took a small, sharp knife and cut them in half. Esther took the halves and put them into a special tool used for squeezing out the juice. Once they had enough juice, the girls added sugar, some Haitian vanilla, and water.

"Grandpa, the juice is ready. Can we do anything else?" asked Marie.

"No thank you. Your mom's rice and beans will be enough."

"It's a good thing this isn't New Year's Day," said Sadrack, "or you would have to fix pumpkin soup."

"I love pumpkin soup," said Esther.

"Umm! When chicken, okra, celery, pumpkin, and spices are mixed together, there's nothing like it," said Marie.

Esther rubbed her tummy. "I'm getting hungry just thinking about it."

Grandpa Lucien cut a mango into chunks and put the pieces on a plate. "You kids can share this," he said.

"By the way," asked Esther, "why do we have pumpkin soup on New Year's Day?"

"I know," said Sadrack. "I learned that in school last year. Haiti gained its independence from France over 200 years ago. We celebrate on New Year's Day."

"I know that," said Esther. "But what does that have to do with pumpkin soup?"

"Well," began Sadrack, "the French were rich. They could have pumpkin soup whenever they wanted it. But the Haitians were slaves. They could never have it."

"When Haiti gained its independence, the people decided to celebrate by eating pumpkin soup," added Marie.

"So that's why we eat it on New Year's Day!" Esther said.

Grandma Yvette groaned, and all the children looked at each other. Grandpa Lucien jumped up and went to check on her. When he returned, the children asked, "Will Grandma be OK?"

"Yes," replied Grandpa. "When I took her to the Nazarene clinic this morning, the nurses tested her blood and gave her some medicine. Then they did something else for your grandma."

"What did they do?" asked Esther.

"They prayed for her."

"Oh, that's good!" said Marie.

Grandpa Lucien nodded. "She'll still be sick for a while though, and she'll need lots of sleep."

"Grandma says, 'Sickness comes on a horse, but leaves walking,'" said Marie.

"That's true. Getting well takes time," agreed Grandpa.

"Where's the clinic?" asked Esther.

"You know," said Sadrack, "it's that building at the bottom of the hill. You go through the big gates, and it's on the right."

"You mean where they park the cars and keep the donkeys?"

"That's it," said Sadrack.

"When did they build the clinic?" asked Esther.

"It was built in 1960," said Grandpa Lucien.

"Did Haitians always work there?" asked Sadrack.

"No, missionaries worked there for many years. But after they trained Haitians to work in the clinic, the missionaries were no longer needed there. Bill Dawson helped them make this change in 1991."

"Wait a minute," said Marie, "I know Bill Dawson."

"Me too," added Esther. "Bill and Martha are nice. They say 'hi' to everybody!" Esther smiled as she remembered the last time she had seen them.

"Where do they live?" asked Sadrack.

"They live in the United States now. But they come back when they can to be sure things in the clinic are OK," answered Grandpa.

"Has the clinic helped lots of people?" asked Esther.

"Yes it has. Besides your grandma, I know many people who have been helped. Not all of them came by donkey or car either."

"Grandpa, tell us a story," encouraged the children.

"Clean your hands and go sit on our new bench. I'm going to check on your grandma again. I'll be right there."

The children cleaned the sticky mango off their hands and then hurried outside to wait on the bench.

"What story should I tell?" asked Grandpa as he joined them.

"You told us not everyone came to the clinic by donkey or car," said Esther. "I know a lot of people walked, but that's not a story."

"Ah, you never know," Grandpa Lucien said. He smiled as he remembered a day long ago. "Krik?" he asked in a soft voice.

4
God Is the Best Doctor

"Krak!" whispered the children.

"Many years ago, a man was trying to walk to the clinic. He had hurt his back and his leg. As he traveled the long and hilly road, he limped in pain. He was trying to get to the clinic before it closed, but . . ."

"He was too slow, right?" Esther interrupted.

"Yes, he needed to rest often. On one of his stops, he began talking with two men who were construction workers. When they saw he was in pain, they knew they had to help him. What could they do? They thought for a minute and came up with an idea. They emptied their wheelbarrow and put the lame man into it. As they wheeled him up the hill to the clinic, they talked to him."

"What did they talk about?" asked Marie.

"Let's see if you can answer that question. When they arrived at the clinic, the man asked a nurse to pray with him. He wanted to be saved."

"I think the workers talked to the man about Jesus," said Sadrack.

"That's a good guess," said Grandpa. "Haitians love telling everyone they meet about Jesus."

"What happened next?" asked Esther.

"The nurse gave the man some medicine. Then the two workers wheeled him all the way home. A

21

week later, the man limped back to the clinic for a checkup. His smile told everyone that he was feeling better on the inside as well as the outside. His friends encouraged him to go to church so he could meet more Christian friends."

"Did he go?" asked Esther.

"Yes, he did. And he told everyone in church that he had a new life. He thanked God for the Church of the Nazarene and the clinic."

"I like that story," said Marie.

"Wait. It's not over yet," said Grandpa.

"What else happened?" asked Sadrack.

"The man told all of the men he worked with about Jesus, and 19 of them decided to become Christians too."

"Wow! That's amazing," said Marie. "Do you know any other clinic stories?"

"There are so many. Let's see. One time, a grandfather rushed into the clinic with his grandbaby over his shoulder."

"What was wrong?" asked Esther.

"No one knew at first. They finally realized that a big seed was stuck in her throat. Dr. LaMare tried to get the seed out with her finger. The little girl didn't like the doctor's finger in her mouth. So she bit her with the only two teeth she had."

"Ouch! Baby teeth can really hurt!" said Sadrack, as he looked at his finger and then at Esther.

"Did the doctor remove the seed?" asked Marie.

"She did. But the baby died anyway."

"Grandpa! What kind of story is that?" asked Sadrack.

"Wait," Grandpa said again. "Everyone at the clinic prayed. The nurses didn't give up hope. Joan Read began to breathe into the little girl's mouth, and

Lois Ford pushed on her chest. They worked together, and soon the baby began to breathe on her own."

"So the baby lived?" asked Esther.

"Yes, God healed her." Grandpa Lucien wiped a tear from his eye. "She grew up knowing that God loved her. Her grandfather often told her about the day she died."

"It was a miracle!" exclaimed Marie.

"And God still works miracles," said Grandpa.

Sadrack did not waste any time asking the next question. "Grandpa, do you know another miracle story?"

"Let me think. Ah, yes, the miracle at Malik."

"What happened?" asked Esther, as she leaned forward on the bench.

"A pastor and his family came to Malik to visit relatives. While they were there, the dad attended meetings here in Port-au-Prince. The mom had meetings in another village. The kids were playing together near the village's new outdoor toilet. It was very deep and had been dug out of solid stone. The cement lid had a hole. Alma Ruth, who was about a year and a half old, was curious. 'What could that big hole be?' she wondered. Her brothers and sisters were busy, so she thought she'd check it out."

"Uh, oh!" said Marie and Sadrack, as they remembered how curious Esther used to be about some things.

"When the older kids were ready to leave, they looked for their sister. 'Alma Ruth, where are you?' they yelled. Suddenly, they knew what had happened. They thought she must be dead. The children screamed and cried. Their grandma came running. The neighbors came running. One of the men broke the cement very carefully. Another man brought a ladder and climbed down into the darkness. He, too, thought Alma Ruth would surely be dead. But she reached up to him as he climbed down the ladder."

"Yeah!" cheered Esther and Marie.

"Was she hurt?" asked Marie.

"Since no one knew for sure, the girl's grandma took her to the hospital. The doctor said she was just fine. People praised God for protecting her."

"I'm sure her brothers and sisters never let Alma Ruth out of their sight again," said Marie.

"That must have been scary," said Esther, "and smelly!"

"I'm glad you never fell into an outdoor toilet!" exclaimed Sadrack.

Esther wrinkled up her nose. "Me too!"

A horn tooted just outside the gate. "Your mom is here with the rice and beans," Grandpa said. "Children, remember that your health is the greatest of riches."

"We will, and we'll pray for Grandma Yvette," said Sadrack.

5
Thank a Teacher

"I hate school!" complained Esther.

"What happened?" asked Grandpa Lucien.

"Nothing. She just had a bad day," said Sadrack. "I'm so glad Grandma is better!"

Marie looked at her grandma who was sitting on the bench with another lady. They had a big Bible laying open across their laps.

"What's Grandma doing?" asked Esther.

"She's teaching her friend to read," answered Grandpa.

"The lady doesn't know how to read?" Sadrack was surprised.

"No, Sadrack. When we were young, most of us couldn't go to school, especially the girls," replied Grandpa Lucien. "The lady is from a small village where many still can't go to school. Her family needs her to help sell vegetables at the market."

The children looked at each other. Suddenly, Marie's eyes opened wide. "Did Grandma go to school?"

"No, she didn't," answered Grandpa.

"But she can read," said Marie.

"She sure can!" said Sadrack. "She reads the Bible all the time."

"How did she learn?" asked Marie.

"She was taught by a friend who was taught by someone else," said Grandpa.

"Who?" asked Marie.

"I don't know. But I do know that missionaries Walt and Linda Crow worked at the mission. Their daughters, Lori and Juli, loved books and knew how to read. They had a Haitian friend, Lucille, who didn't know how to read. So they decided to teach her. Mrs. Crow gave Lori and Juli a beginner's book and some paper. In the afternoons, the girls would sit under the almond tree in the backyard and teach Lucille."

"Did Lucille learn to read?" asked Esther.

"Yes, she learned very well. She taught her sisters and anyone else who wanted to learn."

"But she didn't teach Grandma?" asked Marie.

"No, but everyone who learned to read taught someone else." Grandpa Lucien looked at his wife and smiled. "Your grandma loves to teach others. I'm proud of her."

"Do you think I could teach someone?" asked Esther.

"Yes, you could teach them what you have learned."

"If you want to be a teacher, you better pay attention in class," teased Sadrack.

"I guess I don't hate school," said Esther.

"That's good," said Grandpa Lucien. "But it would be even better if you were thankful for school."

"Thankful for school?" questioned Sadrack.

Grandpa frowned at Sadrack and replied, "Many years ago in 1988, missionaries Bill Dawson and David Taylor were visiting a Nazarene church and its school in Haiti. The church is only about 75 miles from Port-au-Prince. But it took the men several hours to travel over very difficult roads to reach the area.

"As they were about to enter the church, a shy

13-year-old boy introduced himself. When he learned that one of the men was David Taylor, he became excited. The boy asked, 'Are you the one who used to give us food at the school?'

"'Yes, I am,' Mr. Taylor replied.

"The boy smiled and said, 'Thank you! Because of you, I can read.'"

"Why did the boy say that?" asked Esther. "Did Mr. Taylor teach him to read?"

"No, but he was the missionary in charge of building the schools. He was also the director of the lunch program that provided hot, healthy meals for the children. Since the boy was so thankful for a place where he could learn and eat a hot meal, he wanted to tell Mr. Taylor."

"How many schools are there in Haiti?" asked Esther.

"The Church of the Nazarene has 300 schools in Haiti where children can learn to read. They learn about God's love and forgiveness too."

"Now lots of us go to school," said Marie quietly.

"Yes, it's an answer to our prayers," Grandma Yvette said. "And we're so happy that girls can go too," Grandma added, as she gathered a few plastic bags. She and her friend were going to go to the market.

"Have girls always been allowed to go to Nazarene schools?" asked Marie.

"Yes, Nazarenes believe girls need an education too," said Grandpa Lucien. "Did you know that one of the directors of the Bible college was a lady?"

"Really!" said Sadrack. "I didn't know that."

"Yes, there have been many directors since Pastor Paul Orjala was here. Jeanine Van Beek was one of them."

"She taught pastors?" asked Marie.

"Yes, she was a powerful witness for God," said Grandpa Lucien. "Now do your homework, and I may have time to tell you a story about Jeanine before your mother comes. You know one of my favorite proverbs is 'Don't wait until you're sleepy to make your bed.'"

"Don't worry, Grandpa; we'll be prepared for school tomorrow," said Marie.

The children began asking each other questions about what they had learned. They reviewed the information they had memorized at school. Soon they knew their lessons well.

Grandma Yvette and her friend soon returned from the market with some grapefruit and tomatoes. After a snack, Sadrack and his sisters quietly took their places on the bench under the mango tree. Grandpa smiled and asked, "Krik?"

6

Sitting Snake

"Krak!" exclaimed the children.

"Jeanine Van Beek was from Holland. She spoke many languages and was able to learn Creole quickly. Miss Van Beek knew the Bible well. When she was named the director of the Bible college, she wanted to teach the students what she had learned. And she wanted the school to be known for excellence. Do you know the proverb, 'Leading a snake to school is nothing; it's making him sit that's hard?'"

Esther laughed. "Snakes sitting in science class? That's so silly!"

"She must have been a good teacher," said Sadrack.

"Yes," said Grandpa Lucien, "and she protected the school."

"What do you mean?" asked Marie.

"One day, Miss Van Beek looked out her window. She saw a soldier with a gun standing on top of the hill where the college was located. Other soldiers were crawling up the hill on their bellies. They were fighting a practice battle. Miss Van Beek ran out of her house and began yelling at the men. 'This is a Bible college. You cannot be here! You need to leave and not come back to this hill again.' The soldiers said they were sorry, and they never came back to practice there again."

"I don't think I'd yell at a man with a gun," said Marie. "That doesn't seem like a good idea."

"You're right," Grandpa Lucien agreed. "It's not a good idea. But she didn't want the soldiers practicing near the school."

"Did Miss Van Beek protect the students too?" asked Sadrack.

"Yes and no. She prayed for them and tried to make the campus a safe place," said Grandpa. "On the other hand, Miss Van Beek encouraged the students to tell people about Jesus everywhere they went. And sometimes that was dangerous.

"Miss Van Beek thought that Grace Children's Hospital was a great place to share the hope of Jesus. The children at this hospital had a disease that affects the lungs. It's called tuberculosis [tuh-bur-kyuh-LOH-sis]. The Bible college students held services there on Sunday mornings. They played music and sang songs. The students fell in love with these children who were very sick. Some of the children had never had visitors before."

"Grandpa, why did the students enjoy working with these kids?" asked Marie.

"They wanted to share God's love with them. One day, a young mother accepted Jesus as her Savior. In her arms, she held Sandra, her dying baby girl. The students prayed for the baby. Each week, the baby grew stronger. A few months later, Sandra was sent home from the hospital, happy and healthy."

"Wow!" Esther exclaimed. "That's great!"

"Yeah, that's cool!" said Sadrack.

"Yes, it is. However, not all of the children were healed from the disease," said Grandpa. "But many of them accepted Jesus. And not only were the children saved, there were nurses and family members saved too! The children had a new Spirit. The Holy Spirit filled them with hope and gave them a reason to live. They told others about God's love."

"Now I understand why the students wanted to spend time with the kids," said Marie.

"What else did the college students do?" asked Sadrack.

"They played soccer. Their team played against teams from other Bible colleges. They sang songs and learned to play the piano and other instruments. The students grew close to God and to each other, and they had lots of good times."

"Is the school still that way today?" asked Marie.

"Oh, yes! But there have been many directors since Miss Van Beek. I can name a few other missionaries who were directors—Rev. Dave Crofford, Rev. Terry Ketchum, Rev. Scott Stargel, and Rev. Greg Crofford. And now Rev. Bill Dawson is the director. The mission of the school remains the same—to train men and women in Haiti who are called to pastor.

"The campus has changed though," said Grandpa. "Many new buildings have been built by mission teams from around the world. But that story will have to wait. I hear your mom at the gate. I'll see you tomorrow, children."

7
God's World

"Hi, Grandpa. Hi, Grandma. Look what I got in school today," said Sadrack, as he held up a plastic sack.

"Wow! It's a baby tree," said Grandpa Lucien. "What kind is it?"

"It's an orange tree. May I plant it in your yard?"

"Sure, that would be fine," said Grandma Yvette. "I love oranges. You can plant the tree near our wall."

"OK, I'll need a shovel to dig a hole and some water. The teacher showed us just what to do."

"I'll get the shovel from Samson's house," said Marie, as she headed for the gate.

"And I'll get some water," said Esther, running toward the well.

When the girls returned, Sadrack took the shovel and started digging a hole. A tarantula skittered (quickly ran) from the hole in the ground.

Grandpa Lucien laughed. "I remember how some of the missionary kids liked to catch those spiders."

"What did they do with them?" asked Esther.

"Some of the kids kept them as pets," said Grandma Yvette. "Others just let them go. And a few kids put them in clear plastic molds and made paperweights. They sold them to people who were visiting Haiti."

Marie watched as Sadrack continued shoveling the dirt. "I hope a snake doesn't come out of that hole," she said. "Snakes are scary."

"I hate snakes!" said Esther.

"I don't like them either, but at least there are no poisonous snakes in Haiti," said Grandma Yvette. "A missionary kid named Nick Stargel had a snake as a pet. When a snake was discovered in the house of another missionary, Nick was called to come and get it. Nick took the snake home as a friend for the one he already had."

"Boy, he was a brave kid," said Marie.

"Braver than me," added Esther.

When Sadrack was done digging the hole, he removed the plastic from his little tree. He carefully placed it in the hole and held it while Marie pushed in the dirt. Then she lightly patted the dirt around the roots. When the tree was in place, Esther poured water on the ground so the roots would not get thirsty.

"Good job, children," said Grandpa Lucien.

"Why did your teacher give you this tree?" asked Marie.

"Because we learned that trees are important. And after the lesson, our teacher gave each of us a tree to take home and plant."

"Why are trees important?" asked Esther.

"Let's see if I can remember." Sadrack thought for a minute. "They provide shade from the sun on a hot day."

"They give us food to eat," said Grandma Yvette, as she plucked a ripe mango from their tree.

"We burn them to make charcoal for cooking," said Marie.

"Trees draw rain from the clouds," said Grandpa Lucien. "Because so many trees have been cut down, the weather pattern is changing. We get less rain, and everything is so dry."

"Our teacher said that when we cut down a tree, we should plant three more," Sadrack told everyone.

Grandma Yvette nodded. "That's a good idea because some of the newly planted trees won't live."

"Planting trees is fun too," said Esther.

"Trees also help to keep the dirt in place," said Sadrack.

"What?" asked Esther.

"The roots are like little fingers that hold onto the dirt when it rains," explained Sadrack.

Esther looked puzzled. "Why is that important?"

"When the dirt is washed into the ocean, only the rocks are left," said Sadrack.

"And you can't grow food on rocks," added Grandma Yvette.

"That's bad," said Esther.

"Do you remember the flood at Gonaives [goh-nah-EEV] a few years ago?" asked Grandpa Lucien.

"No," replied Esther, "I don't."

"You were too young to remember, but I do. Lots of people died," said Marie sadly.

"Tropical storm Jeanne brought lots of rain," said Grandma Yvette. "It destroyed the area."

"I remember collecting food to send to the people," said Sadrack.

"Yes, many Haitians sent supplies to help them," said Grandpa. "The Bible college students sent food and clothes. And more food and clothes and school supplies were sent from other parts of the world."

"What does all of this have to do with trees?" asked Esther.

"Because there were no trees to hold the dirt in place, there was no dirt to soak up the rain. The water ran very quickly down the mountains, and that's what caused the flood," explained Sadrack.

"Oh, I see," said Esther. "We need to keep our trees. I'm glad our mountain has lots of trees."

"Ah," said Grandpa Lucien with a smile, "that's another story."

"Oh, Grandpa, please tell us the story!" said Sadrack, Marie, and Esther.

"OK. Go wash the dirt off your hands and sit on the bench."

The children ran to do as their grandpa had asked and then waited quietly on the bench.

Grandpa Lucien asked, "Krik?"

8

Busy Hands and Full Stomachs

"Krak!" shouted the children.

"One day, missionary Howard Culbertson's phone rang. A woman on the other end of the line said, 'The National Forestry Service is giving away trees to churches. They want people to plant them next weekend.' Rev. Culbertson told the lady he thought Nazarenes could take about 200 trees. 'Not enough!' she said. 'You need to take at least 1,000 trees.' So he did. Rev. Culbertson called 10 churches. They were excited to help plant the trees.

"The Malik church took 75 trees. On Monday morning, their pastor called Rev. Culbertson to say they wanted 3,000 more trees. The National Forestry Service agreed. The people got busy. When those trees were planted, they asked for 15,000 trees! The government inspectors went to see what was going on. They were happy with what they saw. They sent high school kids to help the church plant their new trees. The Malik church set a goal of covering their mountain with trees."

"So that's why we have so many trees," said Esther.

"Yes," answered Grandpa. "Would you like to hear another story?"

"Yes!" the children agreed.

"Do you know the story about the cows that flew?" asked Grandpa Lucien.

"Cows don't fly," said Sadrack. "That's impossible."

Esther laughed. "That's silly."

"One time, a missionary named Charles Morrow brought several young female cows and two bulls to Haiti," said Grandpa Lucien.

"Why?" asked Marie.

"He wanted to teach pastors how to run a dairy farm. He said it would help them earn a living," explained Grandpa. "But when Mr. Morrow loaded the animals onto the plane in the United States, he forgot something important. You know how the missionaries always use seat belts in their cars?"

"Yes," said Sadrack.

"I have to wear a seat belt when I ride in their cars too," added Marie.

"Good, I'm glad you do. Well, Mr. Morrow forgot the animals' seat belts."

"Grandpa, what would a cow seat belt look like?" asked Esther. She laughed as she pictured it in her mind.

"Animals don't wear seat belts," chuckled Sadrack.

"True, but Mr. Morrow forgot to secure the animals so they couldn't move around in the plane. As the plane went faster and faster down the runway, all of the animals moved to the back of the plane. Since they were very heavy, they caused the tail of the plane to scrape the ground. But it finally lifted into the air."

"Were the animals OK?" asked Esther with a worried look.

"Yes, they were. And during the flight, the missionary pilot figured out how to land safely."

"That was good," said Marie. "Tell us another story."

"Let me think. Hmmm. Missionaries taught people what foods to eat and how to stay healthy. They taught ladies how to crochet [kroh-SHAY] and sew. And they taught men how to fix small engines, repair cars, and manage pig and chicken farms. Pastor Walt Crow taught people how to make plastic coffins (containers used for burying people)."

"Did they use plastic instead of wood to save the trees?" asked Sadrack.

"Exactly!" replied Grandpa.

"Missionaries have sure taught us a lot," said Esther.

"We've also learned how to build churches, homes for pastors, and schools," said Grandma Yvette. "People have come from many different countries to help us."

"Did they all speak Creole?" asked Esther.

"No, but we knew some of the same songs. We sang the songs in Creole, and they sang them in their language. I can remember a verse or two in German."

"Sing for us, Grandpa," begged Marie.

"I thought you wanted another story," teased Grandpa Lucien.

"Oh, all right," said Marie.

"One day, Mr. Dave Blowers took a trip with Rev. Terry Ketchum and a few other missionaries. It was a long trip. They wanted to help build a church at Bois

Brule [BWAH broo-LAY], but they had to see the place first. As they were hiking up the mountain, people started walking with them. These people had something on their heads. Can you guess what it was?"

Esther bounced up and down. "I know, I know. Hair!" Esther laughed, and Grandpa Lucien smiled. Sadrack groaned.

"Besides hair," Grandpa Lucien said. He waited, but the children shrugged their shoulders and shook their heads. "Do you give up?" Grandpa asked.

"Yes," they all said.

"They were carrying cement blocks."

"Cement blocks! Why?" asked Marie.

"The people wanted a church so much that they had already begun to buy the supplies. They had many cement blocks and some tin roofing. Mr. Blowers was surprised and pleased.

"Soon after the missionaries arrived, the rain began. The church people sang, 'The rains came down and the floods came up.' Then they fed their guests a yummy meal."

"What did they eat?" asked Esther.

"You always want to know about food," teased Sadrack.

"I like food," said Esther, as she stuck out her tongue at her brother.

Grandpa answered, "They had carrots, onions, chicken, and flattened fried bananas."

"I love those," said Marie.

"You mean these?" Grandma Yvette held out a small basket of banane pese [BAN-an pay-ZAY]. "Earlier today I made some for you."

"Thank you, Grandma!" Esther took several of the banana chips and began munching happily.

"An empty sack can't stand," Grandma Yvette

said as she smiled. "You're welcome. I'd better let your grandpa finish his story."

"After the group had eaten," continued Grandpa Lucien, "it was time for the missionaries to leave. The people walked down the mountain with them. Along the way, they sang, talked, and laughed. Just before everyone said good-bye, Mr. Blowers prayed for the people of the church. It was a great day."

"Did the people get their church built?" asked Sadrack.

"Yes, they did. Haitian Nazarenes built it. The missionaries taught them how to do the construction work. People danced for joy when a truck brought the pews and pulpit."

"Speaking of trucks," said Grandma Yvette, "I hear your dad's truck."

"I'm expecting a friend to visit me tomorrow, children," said Grandpa Lucien.

"Who?" asked Marie.

"It's a surprise," he replied. "You'll find out."

9
From Here to There

"Is your friend here?" asked Marie, as she hurried through the gate.

"Not yet," said Grandpa Lucien. "He has a long way to come. And he must travel over roads that were washed out by the last tropical storm. What did you children do today?"

"I helped Mom decorate for district assembly," said Sadrack.

"Yeah, our mom and dad are busy getting ready for the meetings. That's why we came here today, even though we didn't have school," said Esther.

"I'm glad you came," said Grandma Yvette. "But how did you get here?"

"We took turns riding the donkey," said Esther.

"Well, not everyone knows how to ride a donkey." Grandpa Lucien chuckled as he remembered some of the trips he had taken.

"They don't?" questioned Marie.

"Why not?" asked Esther.

"In many countries, people don't ride donkeys. They ride in cars," Grandma Yvette explained, "like the ones some of the missionaries drive."

"Yes, that's why many of the missionaries had a tough time riding donkeys at first, but they got used to it," said Grandpa Lucien. "We have many ways to travel in Haiti. Brendan Blowers discovered that while on a big adventure one day."

"Who is he, and what did he do?" asked Sadrack.

"Brendan is an MK. He's Mr. Blower's son," replied Grandpa. His mom asked if he would like to go with his dad to the island of La Gonave [LAH goh-NAHV] for a meeting. It sounded like fun to Brendan. He loved to see new places, so he said 'Yes!' He put on his helmet and then climbed onto the back of his dad's motorcycle. You know how bumpy the road is that leads to the dock. Well, by the time they got there, the poor little guy was sore. But then, they each had to climb onto a man's shoulders. The men carried them to a ferry boat that would take them to the island."

"What did they do with the motorcycle?" asked Sadrack. He loved machines, especially motorcycles.

"After the men got both Brendan and his dad to the boat, they went back for the motorcycle," explained Grandpa. "The trip on the boat took two hours. Parts of it were fun. Brendan liked to watch the flying fish, but he got seasick."

"Yuck!" said Sadrack. He had been on the ferry boat once. He remembered feeling sick, too, as the waves splashed over the side of the boat.

"When Mr. Blowers and Brendan reached the island," Grandpa said, "they continued the trip by motorcycle. By the time they arrived at the meeting, Brendan was very tired and hungry. The people fed him and his dad a good meal. Then Mr. Blowers and the people talked about how the missionaries could help them build a church. Later, Mr. Blowers and his son headed down the mountain in the dark on the motorcycle. The next day, they returned home after an early morning boat ride with high waves that rocked the boat. Brendan decided that he did not want to go on any more adventure trips for a while."

"Did the missionaries ride to the island on the ferry boat too?" asked Sadrack.

"No. Because of all the trips they had to make to the island with building supplies, a group of Nazarenes in the United States bought them their own boat. Their first trip to the island was smooth. After that, the waves became rough and tossed the boat back and forth. But Scott Hannay, the captain, brought the boat safely back to port each time."

"Grandpa, do missionaries always have adventures like that?" asked Marie.

"They try not to," laughed Grandpa, "but things happen. One time, Rev. Greg Crofford, his wife, and Rev. Sadrack Nelson were going to Liancourt to teach a class. Their car broke down near Wahoo Beach. It was a good thing they had a cell phone with them. They called the campus and asked Franz, the mechanic, to bring some tools to help start the car. While they waited, Mrs. Crofford picked up some seashells. Then she and Rev. Crofford taught Pastor Nelson how to play 20 questions."

"We learned how to play that game at church camp," said Marie. "It's fun."

"Yeah, I like it too," added Sadrack.

"Pastor Nelson taught the Croffords how to sing 'Jesus Loves the Little Children' in Creole. And the Croffords taught him how to sing it in English," said Grandpa. "Whenever someone walked by the car, Pastor Nelson explained who they were and what they were doing."

"Why did he do that?" questioned Marie.

"People in the neighborhood were nervous about

having strangers hanging around. Pastor Nelson thought they might not be afraid if they knew what had happened. After he told them, the people always said 'God bless you' and smiled. Finally, Franz arrived and got the car started. Soon they were on their way."

"Our truck breaks down sometimes," said Sadrack. "Once it broke down a mile from home, and we had to walk. That's the good thing about donkeys. They don't break down."

"You know the proverb, 'Close to home is not home,'" said Grandma Yvette.

"My friend should be here very soon," said Grandpa Lucien. "He is traveling on a tap-tap bus."

"I love tap-tap buses!" Esther exclaimed. "They are so colorful, and I like to sit on the benches inside."

Just then, they heard a noise at the gate.

10

New Churches

"Grandpa, he's here!" Marie jumped up and ran to the gate to let the visitor in.

Grandpa looked toward heaven and said a quiet, "Thank You!" Then he went to the gate and shook hands with the tall man who had just entered. "Children, this is Pastor Philippe. He came for the district assembly."

"Are you on our district?" asked Sadrack.

"No, I'm from another district in Haiti," answered the pastor. "But I needed to come to the capital city. And since I have many friends on this district, I decided to come to the meeting here."

"Welcome to Port-au-Prince, Pastor Philippe," said Marie.

"Thank you," replied Pastor Philippe. He settled onto a chair that Grandpa had placed by the story bench. "This is not my first visit. The first time I came here I was a young man. God had called me to be a pastor, and I wanted to come to the Bible college. I came with two shirts, two pair of pants, a big dream, and not much else."

"What happened?" asked Marie.

"I talked to the people at the college, and they accepted me as a student. I worked around the campus cleaning to make money. Later, I became the

pastor of a little church not far from here. When I graduated, I went back to my home area to start new churches. Now my church is a big church. And there are several other churches in my area that we helped to start."

Grandma Yvette brought Pastor Philippe a glass

of citronade. He smiled and thanked her. "My trip took longer than usual, and I am thirsty. This is just what I need," he said.

Marie couldn't wait to ask more questions. "Why do your churches grow so quickly?"

"There are lots of reasons," said Pastor Philippe. "Can you think of some?"

"The church helps people earn money so they can buy food," said Esther.

"You would mention food!" said Sadrack. "I think it's because churches have schools where people can learn to read."

"The church is a good place to meet friends," added Marie.

"All of those reasons are good ones," said Pastor Philippe. "However, the most important reason the churches grow is because people learn about Jesus. When people are afraid, Jesus can give them peace. When they feel alone, He is there with them."

"Another reason is that people invite others to come to church with them," said Grandpa Lucien. "When the ladies go to the market, they tell others about Jesus as they buy their eggplant and zucchini. Men tell their coworkers about the pastor's sermon on Sunday."

"When Christians get sick, they pray to God instead of going to the voodoo leaders," added Pastor Philippe. "They live differently than they did before they were saved, and their neighbors notice. The neighbors become curious. And when they accept an invitation to a service, they are ready for change themselves."

"On Sunday, our pastor said that Jesus is with us wherever we go," said Esther.

"That's right. Haitians have gone many places

around the world, and God is with them," said Grandpa.

"Where have they gone?" asked Sadrack.

"There are Haitian congregations in France, the Dominican Republic, the United States, Mexico, and Canada, to mention a few places," said Pastor Philippe.

"Wow! I'd like to visit some of those churches," said Esther.

"You may get to do that someday. I've been to a church in New York City," said Pastor Philippe. "It was wonderful. The people use the same hymnal that we do. It was like being at home."

"Who do you want to see at district assembly?" asked Sadrack.

"Many of the students I went to the Bible college with are from around here. Some of them traveled together during one summer as an evangelistic team. They had matching outfits and sang and played instruments. When the team arrived in a new town, people took one look at them and knew they wanted to hear what the students had to say. During that summer, the team helped to start 12 new churches."

"That's a lot!" said Esther.

"Yes. And now there are Nazarene churches all over Haiti—north, south, east, and west," said Grandpa Lucien. "There are big churches with thousands of members like the Bel-Air church in downtown Port-au-Prince. And there are small churches like the Ti Coma church."

"And the one on La Gonave!" added Marie.

"Oh, there are lots of churches on that island," said Grandma Yvette. "It's a district all by itself."

"Children, Pastor Philippe needs to rest now," said Grandpa Lucien.

"OK," said Esther, "but I hope we have time to hear more later."

"Remember the proverb, 'A dog has four paws, but walks on one path,'" said Pastor Philippe. "Keep your eyes on Jesus and walk on His path."

11

God Answers Prayer

"Grandpa, what are you doing here at the school?" asked Sadrack, as he ran toward him.

"The way you usually come to our house isn't safe today."

"Why not?" asked Sadrack. "What's wrong?"

"Some men with guns have been stopping people, so we are going home another way."

Grandpa Lucien saw Marie and Esther coming toward them. "Let's not worry the girls by telling them why we're taking another way home," Grandpa suggested. He smiled and put his hand on Sadrack's shoulder as the girls joined them.

"Hi, Grandpa. What are you doing here?" asked Marie.

"We're having an adventure with Grandpa today," said Sadrack quickly.

"Will it be dangerous?" asked Esther. Her eyes were wide with excitement.

"I hope not," said Grandpa Lucien, "but stay close to me."

"OK, we will," said Marie, as she reached for Esther's hand.

When they saw some ladies selling vegetables,

they bought a few tomatoes and some squash for dinner. They passed a little store that sold water and soda. Grandpa bought a King Cola for the children to share. (King Cola does not taste like American cola; it tastes like Juicy Fruit gum.) As they went up a steep hill near Grandpa's house, they heard gunshots.

"Grandpa, who's shooting the gun?" asked Esther.

"Grandpa, is this why we didn't go straight to your house?" asked Marie.

"Yes, I wanted you to be safe, and I didn't want you to worry."

"Well, I am worried!" exclaimed Marie.

"I'm scared!" said Esther.

"There's your grandma. She's looking for us," said Grandpa Lucien. "Quick! Run inside the gate!"

"OK," said the children. They ran as fast as they could. They heard more gunshots fired nearby. Once the children and Grandpa were inside, Grandma shut the metal gate.

"What can we do?" asked Esther with tears in her eyes.

"We can pray for God to keep us safe," said Grandma Yvette.

"But we're just kids," said Marie.

"God listens to children's prayers too," said Grandpa Lucien. "After you pray, I'll tell you a story."

"OK, I'll pray," offered Sadrack. They bowed their heads. "God, thank You for sending Grandpa to pick us up at school today. And thank You for helping us to get here safely. Please keep our parents and our friends safe too."

Everyone said, "Amen." They looked up and smiled at one another.

"Grandpa, now tell us that story," begged Esther.

"Do you remember Brendan Blowers's adventure?" asked Grandpa.

"Yes," said Sadrack. "He was the one who went to La Gonave with his dad."

"Right. When he was eight years old, he prayed a special prayer. He wasn't sure God would answer his prayer. It was not a big important prayer, and he was only a young boy."

"What did he ask God to do?" asked Esther.

"His family was going to move here, and he was going to have to leave his friends. He prayed that God would give him a new friend in his new home. And God did." Grandpa Lucien continued, "About the same time that the Dave Blowers family came here, the Dave Crofford family came. The Croffords had three boys, and Brendan Blowers and Chris Crofford were the same age. They had lots of fun climbing trees, catching tarantulas, riding bikes, and playing on their dads' computers."

"What are they doing now?" asked Marie.

Grandma Yvette answered, "They're both grown up now. Brendan is a missionary, and Chris is in the military. We should pray for them."

"I guess they still like adventure," said Sadrack.

"I have another story about a child's prayer," said Grandpa Lucien. "Kim Read was the daughter of missionaries Terry and Joan Read. One night, she had a dream that her favorite dog, Mitsy, had been poisoned. When she woke up, she found that not only had Mitsy been poisoned, but Mitsy's puppy and brother had also been poisoned. The two dogs died, but the Reads were able to save Mitsy's life by pouring milk down her throat. She became healthy again.

"A short time later, Kim's family went away for the weekend. When they returned, Mitsy was gone.

She had been dognapped. Kim prayed every night for six weeks. She prayed even after her parents had given up hope. She prayed when everyone told her it was hopeless. She just kept praying. One day while in his office, her dad heard a noise. Could it be? Yes! Mitsy had returned. She was skinny, and her fur was ragged. But she was alive, and she had come home. Kim was thrilled. God heard her prayers."

"I like that story," said Marie. "I'm glad that her dog was safe."

"Me too!" added Esther.

"She kept praying, even when it seemed hopeless to other people," said Marie.

"She had faith," said Sadrack.

"We'll have to keep praying for peace in Haiti," said Grandpa Lucien quietly. "Maybe it will return one day."

"Children," said Grandma Yvette, "one of my favorite Haitian proverbs says, 'Beyond the mountain, there is a mountain.'"

"Haiti does have a lot of mountains," said Sadrack.

Marie and Esther had puzzled looks on their faces.

"Yes, but the proverb means more than that." Grandma Yvette smiled. "You may feel small, but behind you is the God who created the universe. Always remember that."

"He loves us," said Esther.

"He listens when we talk," said Sadrack.

"He'll always be with us wherever we are," said Marie.

"Amen," said Grandpa Lucien and Grandma Yvette.